NORTHFIELD BRANCH
446-5990

OCT –   2004

WELCOME TO MY COUNTRY

Welcome to
GERMANY

Gareth Stevens Publishing
MILWAUKEE

Written by
NICOLE FRANK/RICHARD LORD

Designed by
SHARIFAH FAUZIAH

Picture research by
SUSAN JANE MANUEL

First published in North America in 2000 by
Gareth Stevens Publishing
1555 North RiverCenter Drive, Suite 201
Milwaukee, Wisconsin 53212 USA

For a free color catalog describing
Gareth Stevens' list of high-quality books
and multimedia programs, call
1-800-542-2595 (USA) or
1-800-461-9120 (CANADA).
Gareth Stevens Publishing's
Fax: (414) 225-0377.

© **TIMES EDITIONS PTE LTD 2000**
Originated and designed by
Times Editions Pte Ltd
Times Centre, 1 New Industrial Road
Singapore 536196
http://www.timesone.com.sg/te

Library of Congress Cataloging-in-Publication Data
Frank, Nicole.
Welcome to Germany / Nicole Frank and Richard Lord.
p.   cm. -- (Welcome to my country)
Includes bibliographical references and index.
Summary: An overview of the country of Germany that includes
information on geography, history, government, the economy,
people, and lifestyles.
ISBN 0-8368-2496-2 (lib. bdg.)
1. Germany--Juvenile literature. 2. Germany--Description and travel--
Juvenile literature. 3. Germany--Social life and customs--
Juvenile literature. I. Lord, Richard. II. Title III. Series.
DD17.F73   2000
943--dc21   99-39899

Printed in Malaysia

1 2 3 4 5 6 7 8 9 04 03 02 01 00

PICTURE CREDITS
AKG Photo Berlin: 11 (both), 15 (bottom),
    15 (center), 29 (bottom), 30 (top), 32
A.N.A. Press Agency: 15 (top), 19
Axiom Photographic Agency: 1, 7, 35
Susanna Burton: 34
Dave G. Houser Stock Photography: 5, 40,
    43, 45
Hutchison Library: 3 (center), 18
Inter Nationes: 3 (bottom), 10 (both),
    13 (bottom), 16, 17 (right), 29 (top),
    30 (bottom), 31, 33
International Photobank: 26
Life File Photo Library: 21
Photobank Photolibrary/Singapore: 4,
    38 (bottom)
David Simson: 22, 24, 25, 28
Topham Picturepoint: Cover, 2, 6,
    8 (bottom), 9, 12, 13 (bottom), 14,
    17 (left), 20, 36 (both), 37, 39, 41
Travel Ink: 3 (top), 8 (top), 38 (top)
Trip Photographic Library: 23, 27

Digital Scanning by Superskill Graphics Pte Ltd

Contents

Words that appear in the glossary are printed in **boldface** type the first time they occur in the text.

4

Welcome to Germany!

Germany is famous for its contributions to world culture. The country was divided into East Germany and West Germany in 1949 and **reunified** in 1990. Join us on a tour of Germany and learn all about the German people!

Opposite: Many people visit the Marienplatz in Munich. The building on the right is the city hall.

Below: Germans enjoy eating and relaxing at an outdoor café in Berlin.

The Flag of Germany

The current flag was used during many periods in German history. Both East and West Germany have used the same flag, but the East German flag included a **communist** symbol in the center. Reunified Germany kept the West German flag.

5

The Land

Covering an area of 137,802 square miles (357,000 square kilometers), Germany is the third largest country in the European Union, after France and Spain.

Germany has some of the world's most beautiful mountains and rivers. The Harz Mountains make up part of the landscape in central Germany, and the Bavarian Alps lie in southern

Below: The Alps form the border between Germany and Austria. At 9,718 feet (2,962 meters), the highest peak in Germany is Zugspitze.

Left: Hamburg is Germany's largest port. The Alster, Bille, and Elbe Rivers meet in this city, making it an important trading center.

Germany. Large rivers, such as the Rhine, Elbe, Danube, Weser, Oder, and Main, flow across the country.

Northern Germany consists of a broad, flat plain that reaches the North Sea.

Seasons

Germany has a temperate climate with four seasons. The southern Alps experience the coldest temperatures. The **sirocco**, a warm wind from Africa, gives southwestern Germany a mild, comfortable climate.

Above: The Black Forest is a popular holiday destination.

Plants and Animals

Forests cover almost one-third of Germany. The dark fir trees of Baden-Württemberg give the famous Black

Below: This house is surrounded by the spectacular beauty of the Bavarian landscape.

Forest its name. Today, citizens and tourists hike the forest trails to look at the animals and enjoy the scenery.

Germany is home to many animals, including buzzards, hawks, foxes, badgers, elk, and deer. Nature reserves protect much of the land along the former border between East and West Germany. These reserves provide a home for rare animals, such as lynx, wolves, bears, and sea eagles.

Above: The osprey is among the rare bird species that nest in Germany's nature reserves.

History

Not much is known about German history before A.D. 9. In that year, Germanic tribes fought off the Roman army at the Rhine and Danube Rivers. For the next four centuries, the tribes lived alongside the Romans. When the Roman Empire collapsed in 476, a Germanic tribe called the Franks took power. By 700, they had conquered a large part of Western Europe.

Above: Charlemagne, known as Karl der Grosse in Germany, made Latin the official language of the Frankish empire.

From Charlemagne to Bismarck

Charlemagne ruled the Franks from 768 to 814. He expanded the Frankish empire. When he died, the empire was divided among his sons. Power struggles between rulers and with the Catholic Church continued for the next three hundred years.

In 1517, a German monk named Martin Luther posted his complaints about the Catholic Church on a church door. His action led to the **Reformation**,

Above: Martin Luther rejected the Catholic Church and helped create the Protestant **denomination**.

when Christianity split into the Protestant and Catholic denominations. The two groups struggled for power throughout the sixteenth century. The Thirty Years' War (1618–1648) left Germany further divided into many small kingdoms under different rulers.

In 1871, Otto von Bismarck, the prime minister of Prussia (the largest German state) reunified the German kingdoms. Bismarck helped create the German Empire, or Reich (RIKE).

Above, left: Otto von Bismarck was the prime minister of Prussia. He helped create and lead the successful German Empire.

Above, right: King William I of Prussia was the first Kaiser (KYE-zer), or emperor, of the German Empire. Formed on January 18, 1871, the empire lasted forty-seven years.

War and Division

As Germany's power grew, conflicts with other countries arose. From 1914 to 1918, Germany fought World War I against many other nations. The Reich ended with Germany's defeat. A new government was set up, but Adolf Hitler and his National Socialist Party, or the Nazis, seized power in 1933.

Led by Hitler, Germany invaded Poland and, in 1939, Great Britain and France declared war on Germany. The

Above: Under Nazi rule, Brandenburg Sachsenhausen **Concentration Camp** and camps like it were used to contain and kill Jewish people and other selected groups.

Opposite: In 1961, East Germany built the Berlin Wall to keep East Germans from escaping to West Germany. The border between the two countries became known as the Iron Curtain.

United States entered the war against Germany in 1941. On May 8, 1945, Germany surrendered, and the Nazi government collapsed.

After World War II, four countries occupied Germany. In 1949, the zones held by the United States, Great Britain, and France formed democratic West Germany. The zone controlled by the Soviet Union became communist East Germany.

Above: The Berlin Airlift memorial was built to honor people who flew supplies into Berlin in 1948, after the Soviet Union sealed off all land routes to the city.

The Road to Reunification

After World War II, both East and West German economies prospered, but conflicts continued between the two countries. From 1961 to 1989, the Berlin Wall kept the two Germanys divided. In 1989, however, communism collapsed in Europe. The Berlin Wall came down, and Germany reunified on October 3, 1990, amidst much celebration.

Below: On October 3, 1990, Germans celebrated their country's reunification at the parliament building in Berlin.

Louis II (1845–1886)

German-born Louis II was king of Bavaria from 1864 to 1886. He urged Germany's princes to form an empire. In his later years, he withdrew from politics to focus on the arts. In 1886, he was declared insane and later found drowned.

Louis II

Adolf Hitler (1889–1945)

Austria-born Adolf Hitler was the leader of the National Socialist (Nazi) Party. In 1933, he became **chancellor** of Germany. His policies led to World War II and caused much suffering.

Adolf Hitler

Konrad Adenauer (1876–1967)

Konrad Adenauer began his political career in 1906. Under the Nazis, he was sent to a concentration camp. He reentered politics after the war, becoming the first chancellor of West Germany in 1949.

Konrad Adenauer

Government and the Economy

Germany is a democratic republic with two houses of parliament — the *Bundestag* (boon-des-TAHG), consisting of elected representatives, and the *Bundesrat* (boon-des-RAHT), made up of appointed lawmakers. Germany has sixteen states, each with its own elected parliament.

Below: Under the party system, each voter has two votes, one for a political party and one for a specific candidate.

Leading Germany

All German citizens over the age of eighteen have the right to vote. The main political parties in Germany include the Christian Democratic Union (CDU), the Social Democratic Party (SDP), and the Green Party.

As the head of the Bundestag's majority party, the chancellor is the most powerful person in Germany. Parliament elects the president, whose role is largely **ceremonial**.

Above, left: In 1994, Claudia Nolte became the Minister for Family, Senior Citizens, Women, and Youth.

Above, right: Helmut Kohl (*pictured*) became the first chancellor of reunified Germany in 1990. In 1998, Gerhard Schroeder replaced Kohl as chancellor.

A Thriving Economy

Since the 1960s, Germany has ranked as the third largest economy in the world. It exports electronics, cars, and food to countries all over the world. The German currency is the Deutsche mark, but it will soon be the Euro, the new European Union currency.

Transportation

Germany's efficient transportation system includes thirteen airports and a

Below: German **industrialization** began in the early 1800s in the Ruhr Valley. Today, more than a third of Germany's labor force is involved in manufacturing.

Left: Germany's rivers have always been important for trade. River cruises are a fun way to sightsee!

network of railroads and subways. The **Autobahn** (AW-to-bahn), Germany's system of highways, is world famous.

On the Job

Germans work hard and enjoy about six weeks of paid vacation a year. Labor unions guard the welfare of employees.

People and Lifestyle

About 82 million people live in Germany. Most of their ancestors came from other parts of Western Europe.

Germans are proud of the regions in which they were born. Their overall German identity often comes second,

Left: These young children are wearing the regional dress of Bavaria. Traditional outfits are now used mainly for special occasions.

after their identity as Bavarians, Saxons, Swabians, Hessians, or East Friesians.

People from different regions in Germany tend to have different **traits**. Northerners are often tall, blond, and blue-eyed, while southerners can be darker and shorter. Accents, **demeanor**, and dress can also vary by region.

Below: Turks, Italians, Greeks, Spaniards, Moroccans, and citizens of the former Yugoslavia make up the largest groups of foreigners in Germany.

About seven million immigrants live in Germany. Many originally came from other European countries and from Asia. The city of Frankfurt has the largest immigrant population.

Family Life

German families rarely have more than two children. Larger households are more common in the countryside than in the cities. Both parents usually work to support the family.

Germans love traveling. Many families take short vacations abroad during the school holidays.

Left: Dogs and other house pets are treated like members of the family in Germany.

Opposite: German families decorate trees and open gifts on Christmas Eve.

23

Education

All students attend school together until the fifth grade, when they are tested and divided according to the results. The *Hauptschule* (HOWPT-shool-uh) trains pupils for jobs in trade and industry, the *Realschule* (ray-AHL-shool-uh) prepares them for mid-level jobs, and the *Gymnasium* (gim-NAH-zee-oom) prepares them for a university and executive-level jobs.

Below: Lessons are conducted in German. Many pupils study English as a second language.

The school day lasts from early morning until noon in Germany. Schools do not have sports teams or other activities, so students pursue their leisure interests by joining clubs and other community organizations.

Each state runs its own schools. About 5 percent of children attend private schools. About 25 percent of students attend a university. Students help decide how the university is run.

Above: Students take the bus home after school. All German children must attend school for at least nine years. Gymnasium students go to school for thirteen years.

Religion

Freedom of religion is strictly protected in Germany. About 28 million people are members of the Lutheran Church, and about 30 million belong to the

Left: Artist Marc Chagall designed the colorful stained glass windows of St. Stephen's Church in Mainz.

Roman Catholic Church. Despite their large numbers, only 5 percent of Lutherans and 19 percent of Catholics go to church regularly. Public schools offer religion classes. Church members

pay a tax to the government to help support the work of the Church.

Islam is Germany's largest minority religion. Other religious faiths in Germany are Judaism, Methodist, and Baptist.

Above: More than two million Muslims, mostly Turkish, live in Germany.

Language

Did you know that English began as a German **dialect** and developed into a separate language over time? This is why, even now, the German and English languages share many similarities.

Pronouncing German words is not hard once you know the main differences between German and English — Germans pronounce the letter *W* like the English *V* and pronounce the letter *V* like the English *F.*

Literature

German literature began with the legends of German gods and heroes. During the 1400s, Martin Luther translated the Bible into German. The invention of the printing press popularized the German language. In the eighteenth century, German author Johann Wolfgang von Goethe wrote

Below: German and English belong to the same family of languages.

Faust, the story of a man who sells his soul to the devil in return for all the knowledge in the world.

Other famous German writers include Thomas Mann, Bertolt Brecht, Herman Hesse, Günter Grass, and Heinrich Böll.

Above: Günter Grass wrote many works about the hardships Germans faced during World War II.

Left: "Hansel and Gretel" is a popular fairy tale collected and written down by the Brothers Grimm in the 1800s.

Arts

Germany has made many contributions to the arts, and Germans describe themselves as a *Kulturvolk* (kool-TOOR-fulk), or "a people of culture."

You may be familiar with some of Germany's great composers. You may even have played music written by Bach, Brahms, Handel, Beethoven, or Schumann.

Above: The works of classical composer Ludwig van Beethoven (1770–1827) are famous throughout the world.

Left: German children are encouraged to study music. Today, there are about two hundred orchestras in Germany.

Painting and Sculpture

Early German art focused mainly on religious themes. The late 1400s and the 1500s produced renowned German artists, such as Albrecht Dürer and Hans Holbein the Younger. The pain and loss of the World Wars were common twentieth-century themes. Today, Germany has more than 1,500 museums and art galleries. Works of art are also displayed in public spaces.

Architecture and Theater

The earliest examples of German architecture were the cathedrals of the ninth century. From the mid-1600s, beautiful castles were built in the **baroque** style in Germany.

From the 1920s, architects brought simple designs to ordinary buildings, such as factories and offices.

After World War II, cities had to be rebuilt as quickly as possible. Therefore, German architects emphasized plainness and **function** rather than style.

Left: Architect Walter Gropius designed this building, with its simple lines. Gropius favored designs for ordinary people, not for the rich.

In the 1920s, Berlin theater reached
a high point with the work of poet/
playwright Bertolt Brecht and director
Max Reinhardt. However, many artists
left Germany when the Nazis took power.

Leisure

People of all ages join clubs, called *Vereine* (fur-INE-hun), in Germany.

With more than 300,000 registered clubs in the country, there is a club for just about anything — bike riding, stamp collecting, dog breeding, and more! Since German schools do not offer recreational activities, sports clubs are extremely popular. One-third of all Germans belong to a sports club.

Above: Germans take part in a street parade. This float was made by members of a club.

The Beautiful Outdoors

Germany's forests and mountains attract many hikers. Rock climbing and skiing are other favorite hobbies.

Left: Members of a soccer club pose for a picture after a game.

Top of Their Game

Soccer, or *Fussball* (FOOS-ball), is Germany's most popular sport. The West German team won the World Cup in 1954, 1974, and 1990.

Famous German athletes include ice skater Katarina Witt, Tour de France winner Jan Ulrich, and tennis players Boris Becker and Steffi Graf. All four have achieved international success in their sports.

Opposite: Soccer player Jurgen Klinsmann celebrates a goal.

Below, left: At the age of seventeen, Boris Becker won the Wimbledon singles title.

Below, right: Steffi Graf was at the top of women's tennis for ten years.

Festivals

Germany celebrates its biggest festival, *Karneval* (KAHR-neh-vahl), or Carnival, in February. Karneval marks the beginning of Lent, the forty-day period of fasting before Easter.

Above: Karneval participants wear colorful masks and costumes.

Left: The bright lights of Oktoberfest light up the city of Munich.

German festivals attract both locals and tourists. Many celebrations center around farming events. Munich's Oktoberfest is a huge beer festival held every October. In November, the Rhineland celebrates its grape harvest.

Left: Traditional dancers perform at a festival in southern Germany.

Christmas festivities begin well before December 25. In the cities, street markets inspire people to get into the Christmas spirit. On Christmas Eve, families gather for a big celebration.

Food

Germans love good food. The main meal is served in the middle of the day. Dinner tends to be a lighter meal, consisting of bread, cold cuts, cheese, and salad.

In the late afternoon, people eat rolls and cakes with coffee or tea. Children enjoy hot chocolate or fruit juice instead of coffee.

Below: Pretzels are a favorite German food.

Left: Did you know that hot dogs, or frankfurters, originally came from the city of Frankfurt?

Delicious Dishes

Favorite German foods include potatoes, sauerkraut (a pickled cabbage), and apple strudel (a dessert made with apples, raisins, and ground almonds). *Schnitzel* (SHNIT-tsuhl) is a breaded pork cutlet. German *Wurst* (VORST), or sausage, is made with pork and other meats.

As the Germans say, "*Guten Appetit*" (GOO-ten upp-eh-TEET), or "Enjoy your meal!"

GERMANY

SWEDEN

DENMARK

BALTIC SEA

1

NORTH SEA

SCHLESWIG-
HOLSTEIN

MECKLENBURG-
WESTERN POMERANIA

● Hamburg

POLAND

● Bremen

Elbe

2

Weser

LOWER SAXONY

Oder

■ BERLIN

THE NETHERLANDS

NORTH
RHINE-WESTPHALIA

BRANDENBURG

SAXONY-ANHALT

● Wittenberg

HARZ MTS

Elbe

SAXONY

*Ruhr
Industrial
Area*

THURINGIA

3

BELGIUM

Bonn ●

Rhine

HESSE

RHINELAND-
PALATINATE

● Frankfurt

Main

CZECH
REPUBLIC

LUXEMBOURG

SAARLAND

BAVARIA

Bavarian Forest

4

FRANCE

Rhine

Black Forest

● Stuttgart

Danube

BADEN-
WÜRTTEMBERG

● Munich

AUSTRIA

BAVARIAN ALPS

*Zugspitze
(9,718 feet/2,962 m)*

5

――	**International Boundary**
―	**State Boundary**
■	**Capital**
●	**City**
〜	**River**

SWITZERLAND

ITALY

42

Above: Street musicians play for passersby in a plaza in Frankfurt.

Austria D5

Baden-Württemberg
  B4
Bavaria C4
Bavarian Alps C5
Bavarian Forest
  C4–D4
Belgium A3
Berlin C2
Black Forest B4–B5
Bonn A3
Brandenburg C2-D2
Bremen B2

Czech Republic
  D3–D4

Danube C4
Denmark B1–C1

Elbe River C2–C3

France A4
Frankfurt B3

Hamburg B2
Harz Mountains C3
Hesse B3

Italy C5

Lower Saxony B2
Luxembourg A4

Main River C3
Mecklenburg-
  Western
  Pomerania C2
Munich C4

Netherlands A2
North Rhine-
  Westphalia B2-B3

Oder River D2

Poland D2

Rhine River B3-B4
Rhineland-Palatinate
  A3-B3
Ruhr Industrial
  Area A3

Saarland A4
Saxony C3–D3
Saxony-Anhalt C3

Schleswig-Holstein
  B1–B2
Stuttgart B4
Sweden C1–D1
Switzerland B5

Thuringia C3

Weser River B2
Wittenberg C3

Zugspitze C5

Quick Facts

Official Name   Bundesrepublik Deutschland, Federal Republic of Germany

Capital   Berlin

Seat of Government   Bonn

Official Language   German

Population   82 million

Land Area   137,802 square miles (357,000 sq. km)

States   Baden-Württemberg, Bavaria, Berlin, Brandenburg, Bremen, Hamburg, Hesse, Lower Saxony, Mecklenburg-Western Pomerania, North Rhine-Westphalia, Rhineland-Palatinate, Saarland, Saxony, Saxony-Anhalt, Schleswig-Holstein, Thuringia

Highest Point   Zugspitze 9,718 feet (2,962 m)

Major Rivers   Elbe, Main, Rhine

Major Mountains   Bavarian Alps, Harz Mountains

National Anthem   "Das Deutschland Lied" ("The Germany Song")

Currency   Deutsche mark (DM 1.81 = U.S. $1 in 1999)

Opposite: Berlin's Charlottenburg Palace was once the summer home of Prussian kings.

Glossary

Autobahn (AW-to-bahn): a network of highways stretching over 6,835 miles (11,000 kilometers) in Germany.

baroque: a style in architecture and art of the early seventeenth to mid-eighteenth century. The baroque style is marked by ornate patterns that suggest movement.

Bundesrat (boon-des-RAHT): the house of appointed lawmakers in the German parliament.

Bundestag (boon-des-TAHG): the house in the German parliament consisting of 672 elected representatives.

ceremonial: relating to formal requirements rather than having political authority.

chancellor: the leader of the German government.

communist: relating to a political movement based on the ideas of German philosopher Karl Marx. Under communism, all property belongs to the community or state.

concentration camp: a guarded compound for the confinement of political prisoners. An estimated six million people, many of them Jews, died in Nazi concentration camps during World War II.

demeanor: appearance, attitude, and behavior.

denomination: a religious organization that unites numerous congregations.

dialect: a regional variety of a certain language.

function (n): a certain type of duty.

Gymnasium (gim-NAH-zee-oom): a school that prepares students for university studies and executive positions in industry and commerce.

Hauptschule (HOWPT-shool-uh): a school that prepares students for jobs in trade and industry.

industrialization: the act of building factories and introducing manufacturing on a large scale.

Realschule (ray-AHL-shool-uh): a school that prepares students for mid-level jobs in business and public service.

Reformation: the sixteenth-century movement for change in the Roman Catholic Church.

reunified: joined together again.

sirocco: a warm wind from Africa.

traits: characteristics.

More Books to Read

Berlin. Cities of the World series. Richard Conrad Stein (Children's Press)

The Berlin Wall. New Perspectives series. R. G. Grant (Raintree/Steck Vaughn)

Christabel Bielenberg and Nazi Germany. History Eyewitness series. Christabel Bielenberg and Jane Shuter (editor) (Steck Vaughn)

Germany. Michael S. Dahl (Bridgestone)

Germany. Festivals of the World series. Richard Lord (Gareth Stevens)

Germany. Major World Nations series. Sean Dolan (Chelsea House)

If I Lived in Germany... Roseanne Knorr and John Knorr (illustrator) (Longstreet Press)

Introducing Bach. Famous Composers series. Ronald Vernon (Silver Burdett)

The Rise of the Nazis. New Perspectives series. Charles Freeman (Raintree/ Steck Vaughn)

Understanding the Holocaust. George Feldman and Linda Schmittroth (editors) (U*X*L)

Videos

Germany. (Ivn Entertainment)

Germany. (Madacy Entertainment)

Germany: Munich and Bavaria, Berlin and Potsdam. (Questar)

Web Sites

library.advanced.org/18802/gazette.htm

hoshi.cic.sfu.ca/cgi-bin/cia.pl?Germany

fotw.digibel.be/flags/de.html

ftp.std.com/obi/Fairy.Tales/Grimm/

Due to the dynamic nature of the Internet, some web sites stay current longer than others. To find additional web sites, use a reliable search engine with one or more of the following keywords to help you locate information on Germany. Keywords: *Beethoven, Berlin Wall, Brothers Grimm, Adolf Hitler, Helmut Kohl, Munich.*

Index